Phil Hablitzel
June 19, 1961

AN ATLAS OF AFRICA

AN ATLAS OF AFRICA

by

J. F. HORRABIN

FREDERICK A. PRAEGER, Publishers
NEW YORK

BOOKS THAT MATTER

Published in the United States of America in 1960
by Frederick A. Praeger, Inc., Publishers
64 University Place, New York 3, N. Y.

Second printing, 1961

Library of Congress catalog card number: Map 60-11

AN ATLAS OF AFRICA
is published in two editions:
    A Praeger Paperback (PPS-37)
    A clothbound edition

Printed in the United States of America

PREFACE

THIS BOOK IS NOT intended for the specialist. Its aim is to provide for the intelligent newspaper-reader a summary of some of the key facts about one of the great "burning problems" of today. Nor does it pretend to be objective. It has been drawn and written in the fixed conviction that Europeans—and Americans—owe Africans a big debt; and that the doctrine of *apartheid* and the "*colon* mentality" are uncivilised, un-Christian and altogether damnable. It emphasises the historical background because that background is helping to shape the point of view of educated Africans today; and it is important that we should understand their point of view.

I want to express my thanks for generous help received from Basil Davidson (who will probably groan with pain at the inadequacy of my pre-history), M. Akram Bayatti, Austen Albu, M.P., Sir Leslie Plummer, M.P., and Dr. Anthony Michaelis (for stimulating suggestions). Also to my wife and to Dorothy Davies for their invaluable help in preparing the text.

J. F. H.

Hendon, London, N.W.4.
April, 1960

To colleagues

RITA HINDEN

CREECH JONES

LEONARD BARNES

and

to the memory of

NORMAN LEYS

CONTENTS

11

PART III. TOMORROW

PART I
BACKGROUND

MAP 1

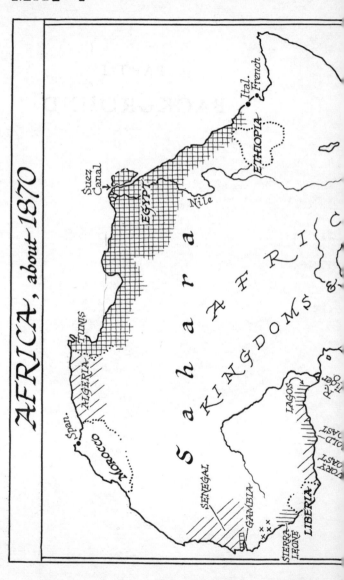

AFRICA, about 1870

Suez Canal

Nile

Ital. French

ETHIOPIA

EGYPT

Sahara

AFRICA

KINGDOMS &

Tunis

ALGERIA

Span.

MOROCCO

SENEGAL

GAMBIA

SIERRA-LEONE

LIBERIA

LAGOS

IVORY COAST

GOLD COAST

R. Niger

J.F.H.

Sultanate of ZANZIBAR

MADAGASCAR

R. Zambesi

MOZ. ZAMBIQUE

R. Limpopo

N

CHIEFDOMS

TRANSVAAL

ORANGE F.S.

NATAL

Orange R.

CAPE COLONY

R. Congo

ANGOLA

England & Wales
on same scale

British ....

French ....

Dutch (Boer) .....

Portuguese ....

Turkish
suzerainty

BEFORE THE "SCRAMBLE"

UNTIL ABOUT three-quarters of a century ago Africa, excepting its Mediterranean shore and the many scattered European trading-stations and occasional small settlements on its long ocean coastline, remained cut off, isolated, from the rest of the world. It was the Dark Continent. South of the great Sahara barrier its very shape was unknown to Europeans until, four centuries earlier, Portuguese seamen crept along its coast southward to find a way to India. Men sailed west across the Atlantic, and discovered (and peopled) a New World; and still "the Africa of the Atlantic slept on." As an eminent historical-geographer[1] wrote—"Africa lies on the surface of the ocean, a huge torso of a continent, headless, memberless, inert. Here is no diversity of form, no fructifying variety of geographical conditions. Humanity has forgotten to grow in its stationary soil."

That is not exactly true, as the archaeologists (*cf.* Maps 5 and 48) have now shown us. Humanity *did* grow in Africa, even though adverse geographical conditions and isolation from other cultures retarded full development. But it is broadly true that, until the last quarter of the 19th century, Africa had no place on the world-map. Then, when the countries of Western Europe began their "Great Scramble," competing with one another for huge slices of African territory, she perforce played the part of a passive victim.

[1] Ellen Semple, *Influences of Geographical Environment.*

18

Let us begin our story with two maps illustrating this opening of the modern chapter of African history, going back afterwards to the preceding stages.

Map No. 1 shows Africa—as known to, and in contact with, Europeans—in the 1870s. The north-eastern corner of the continent—Egypt, Tripoli, and the Red Sea coast—was part of the Turkish Empire. French, Portuguese, and British had established themselves at various points on the coast, west, east and south; their "influence" extending but a few miles into the hinterland. The French had already begun to colonise Algeria, and the Dutch had pushed north from the Cape, away from British rule, and established the two Boer republics. American philanthropists had purchased a piece of territory (Liberia) on the west coast and peopled it with freed slaves, as the British had done in Sierra Leone. Abyssinia (Ethiopia) and Morocco had kept a precarious independence. The vast interior of the continent was "empty."

That is, it contained only Africans.

MAP 2

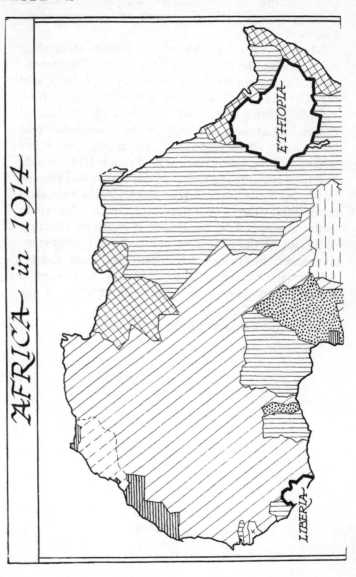

THE GREAT SCRAMBLE

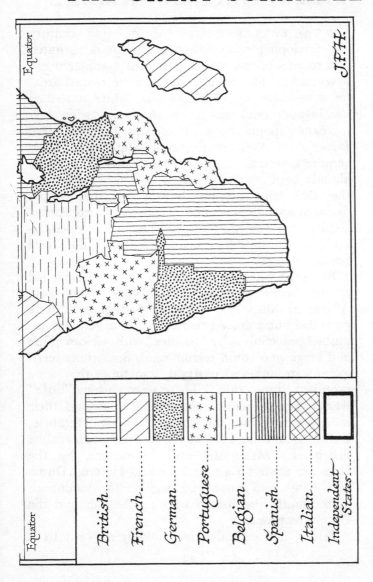

J.F.H.

British..............
French..............
German..............
Portuguese..............
Belgian..............
Spanish..............
Italian..............
Independent States..............

THE GREAT SCRAMBLE

BY THE LATTER quarter of the 19th century fast-developing industrialism in Europe necessitated new sources of raw materials for the manufacturers, new markets for the merchants, undeveloped areas for investment by the financiers, while statesmen sought additional supplies of staple foods for their increasing populations. Thus was born Modern Imperialism. Western European States must needs acquire Overseas Empires. Large parts of Asia had already been seized. The New World of America—the descendants of its European settlers, that is—had declared its independence. There remained Africa. Explorers and missionaries had begun the "opening-up" process. So, Africa being defenceless, the Great Scramble began.

By 1914, when the European Powers quarrelled among themselves and the First World War began, Africa, as Map No. 2 shows, had been entirely parcelled out amongst them. It was largely accomplished peacefully—by "treaties" with African chiefs and kings who could seldom read. Sometimes territories were annexed outright, sometimes they were promised "protection." There were various "little" wars, when Africans vainly tried to defend their independence; by the British against Matabele, Zulus, Ashantis and Sudanese, by the French against Senegalese, Malagasies and Moroccans, by the Germans against East Africans and Hereros. Dutch and British had fought one another for dominance in the south, the British winning the war and the Dutch the peace.

Britain had extended her hold northward from

the Cape to beyond the Zambesi and southward from Egypt (taken over from the Turks). There were visions of an all-British Cape to Cairo railway. France had pressed eastward from Senegal and Guinea across the whole breadth of Sahara and Sudan. The two "new" European Powers, Italy and Germany, had joined in the Scramble. Italy had ousted Turkey from Tripoli (Libya) and secured two areas on the borders of Ethiopia, having failed in an attempt to conquer that country. Germany held four areas, west and east. Little Belgium, whose King Leopold had backed Stanley's exploration of the Congo basin, ruled a vast area in the middle of the continent.

Now, indeed, Africa figured on the world map.

MAP 3

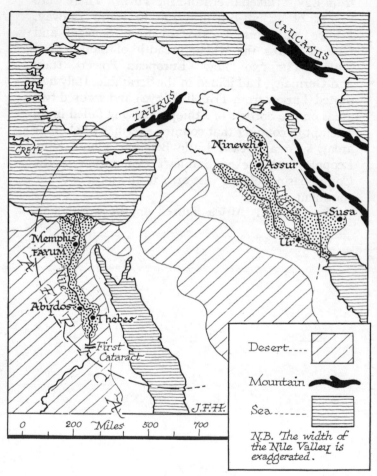

CAUCASUS

TAURUS

CRETE

Nineveh

Assur

Euphrates

Tigris

Susa

Ur

Memphis
FAYUM

Nile

Abydos

Thebes

First
Cataract

J.F.H.

Desert ....

Mountain

Sea ....

| 0 | 200 | Miles | 500 | 700 |

N.B. The width of
the Nile Valley is
exaggerated.

24

CRADLES OF
CIVILISATION

WE GO BACK 6000 years, to the first beginnings of any recorded African history. Western civilisation began in the fertile valleys of the Nile, in north-east Africa, and of the Tigris and Euphrates, in western Asia—two areas not far distant from one another; in a single "region," though academically classified as in different continents. Why were men here able to make the technological and social advances which formed the basis of civilised life? Why in Egypt rather than anywhere else in Africa? Why, having taken root here, did not civilisation spread over the rest of Africa—instead of north and west to Europe?

The brief answer is:—favourable geographical conditions. In the Nile Valley there was exceptionally fertile soil, which the seasonal flooding of the river not merely kept fertile, but made its extension possible by man-made irrigation. This entailed a more and more highly organised society. "The exploitation of the Nile Valley," says Gordon Childe, "required exceptionally close social co-operation." Secondly, natural protection against marauders and invaders was provided by the surrounding desert. Egypt, in effect, was a long, narrow island, cut off by natural barriers from the rest of the world. It was these barriers which hindered the spread of Egyptian civilisation to the great mass of the continent; and it was this isolation which kept that civilisation relatively static for so many centuries.

MAP 4

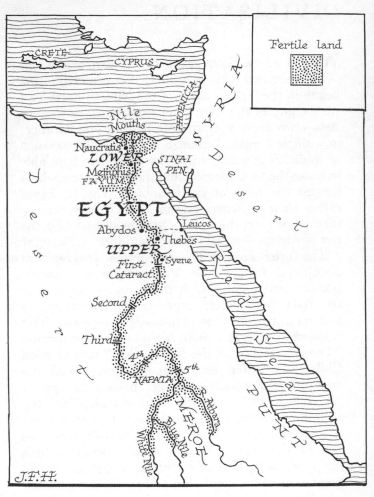

Fertile land

CRETE

CYPRUS

PHOENICIA

SYRIA

Nile
Mouths

Naucratis
LOWER
SINAI
PEN.
Memphis
FAYUM

Desert

EGYPT

Abydos
Leucos
Thebes
UPPER
Syene
First
Cataract

Second

Third

4th
5th
NAPATA
MEROE
R. Atbara
Blue Nile
White Nile

Desert

Red Sea

PUNT

J.F.H.

ANCIENT EGYPT

W E H A V E N O S P A C E here for even a brief summary of Egyptian history. The first Pharaoh reigned
in the 5th millennium B.C. Since its conquest by
Alexander the Great (4th century B.C.) Egypt, until
our own day, has never been ruled by Egyptians—
Greeks, Romans, Arabs, Turks, French and British
have succeeded each other as governments in the
Nile Valley.

Egypt's natural isolation, as we have seen, limited
the influence of its civilisation on the rest of Africa.
When men learned navigation they carried that
influence from the Nile mouth across the Mediterranean to the island of Crete. But it spread only
slowly and weakly from Upper Egypt up the river
to Napata and Meroë, and along the Red Sea coast.
And archaeologists are still debating how far (and
how much) it was carried westward across the
Libyan desert to the (then) fertile areas in the
Sahara.

One point, in view of certain current attitudes to
Africans, should be emphasised. The ancient
Egyptians were not mentally or in any other respect
superior to other Africans. They achieved what they
did because of exceptionally favourable geographical
conditions at a particular stage of social development.

MAP 5

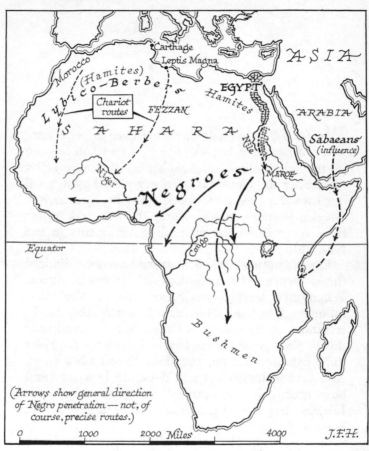

Morocco

(Hamites)

Lybico-Berbers (Hamites)

Carthage
Leptis Magna

ASIA

EGYPT

Hamites

ARABIA

Chariot
routes

FEZZAN

S A H A R A

Nile

influence

Sabaeans
(influence)

Niger

MEROE

Negroes

Congo

Equator

Bushmen

(Arrows show general direction
of Negro penetration — not, of
course, precise routes.)

0   1000   2000 Miles   4000   J.F.H.

28

FIRST STEPS FROM BARBARISM

WHAT OF THE rest of Africa while civilisation was developing in Egypt? The archaeologists are only now beginning to trace the social evolution of the continent—the advance, varying greatly in different regions, from primitive barbarism to the Neolithic stage, with agriculture and stone tools, and, later, the use of iron and the appearance of stone buildings.

The map attempts to summarise some broad facts about three or four millennia B.C. Hamitic peoples occupied the northern part of the continent (parts of the Sahara were then fertile).

The Negroes had entered Africa from Asia about 6000 or 5000 B.C. and were spreading westward and southward. Bushmen, probably the continent's original inhabitants, were being pushed further and further south. The Phoenicians (see next map) established their colonies on the Mediterranean in the 1st millennium B.C. and their influence spread across the Sahara—stone engravings of this date showing wheeled chariots have been discovered.

On the eastern side of the continent Sabaean culture percolated down the coast from southern Arabia as far as Tanganyika, this also at some time in the 1st millennium B.C. or early centuries A.D.

MAP 6

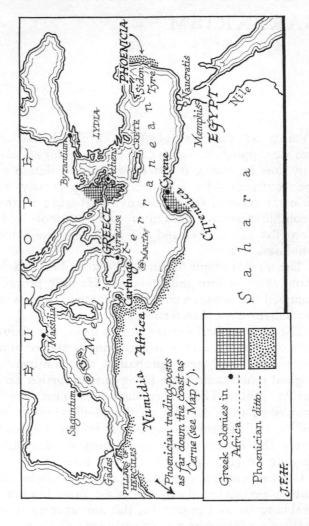

Legend:
- Greek Colonies in Africa ●
- Phoenician ditto ----

Phoenician trading-posts as far down the coast as Carne (see Map 7).

J.F.H.

PHOENICIANS AND GREEKS

ONE MIGHT CALL the Phoenicians the first colonialists. After the collapse of Cretan dominance in the eastern Mediterranean (12th century B.C.) they sailed from their home bases of Sidon and Tyre, established themselves in Malta and Sicily, then on the northern coast of Africa, and finally out through the Pillars of Hercules to Gades, in Spain, and Cerne, down the Atlantic coast of Africa. Their main base later was Carthage, in what is now Tunisia, and their settlements extended along almost the whole of the western Mediterranean African coast.

At this time, too, colonies were founded by the Greek city-states in Cyrenaica, opposite the mainland of Greece on the north side of the sea.

Ever since this period Mediterranean Africa has been more closely linked with southern Europe than with Africa south of the Sahara.

MAP 7

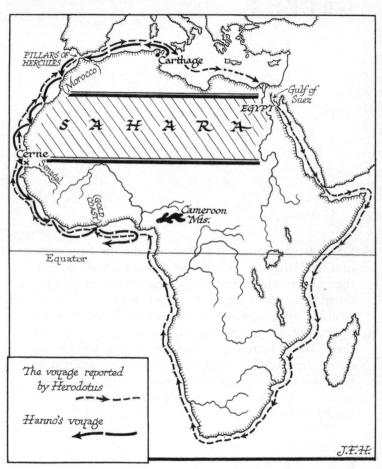

PILLARS OF
HERCULES

Morocco

Carthage

Gulf of
Suez

EGYPT

S A H A R A

Cerne

Senegal

GOLD
COAST

Cameroon
Mts.

Equator

The voyage reported
by Herodotus

Hanno's voyage

J.F.H.

THE FIRST CIRCUMNAVIGATION

About 596 b.c. Phoenician sailors, under orders from Pharaoh Necho of Egypt, set sail from the Gulf of Suez, down the Red Sea, and returned three years later to the Nile mouth through the Pillars of Hercules, having circumnavigated the continent of Africa. Each year, according to Herodotus, they had landed for three months, and grown and harvested a crop. The Cape was not rounded again for 2000 years.

Something under a century later Hanno, a Carthaginian admiral, sailed westward from Carthage with a fleet of 60 ships, carrying 30,000 people, men and women, and established colonies at various points along the African Atlantic coast as far south as Cerne. He took interpreters aboard at each stopping-place, and sailed on until his men were alarmed by the sight of the Cameroon mountain in eruption. Most probably he made one landing on what was later called the Gold Coast (now Ghana).

MAP 8

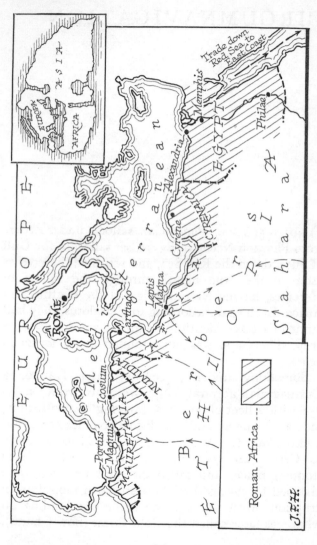

THE ROMANS IN AFRICA

When the Romans finally destroyed Carthage
in the Third Punic War (146 B.C.) they were on the
way to becoming masters of the Mediterranean.
They invented a slogan, "*Mare Nostrum*," which
Mussolini revived some 2000 years later. Imperial
Rome continued what Republican Rome had begun.
Under the Emperor Aurelian (3rd century A.D.) all
the African coastlands north of the Sahara, from
Mauretania (Morocco) to Egypt, were under
Roman rule. "Africa" was the province in the centre
(now Tunisia and the western half of Libya). South
of the provinces was "Ethiopia." From it, says Sir
Mortimer Wheeler,[1] "the cities of the coastal
fringe received the products of the interior—ivory,
precious stones, gold-dust, ostrich feathers, slaves . . .
and above all, animals for the amphitheatres of
Rome and elsewhere." This caravan trade made a
great step forward when the camel was introduced
in the 3rd century A.D.

Sir Mortimer Wheeler also reports evidences of
Roman traders down the East Coast (e.g. the
finding of Roman coins of different periods in
Kenya).

Inset is a map of the world by a Roman geographer showing an Africa much reduced in size,
with the southern end of the Red Sea co-terminous
with the "furthest south" of the continent.

[1] *Rome Beyond the Imperial Frontiers.*

MAP 9

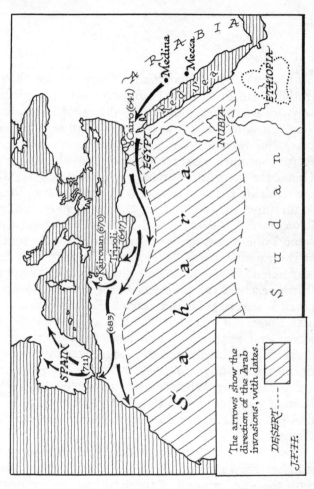

The arrows show the direction of the Arab invasions, with dates.

DESERT -----

J.F.H.

THE COMING OF ISLAM

MUHAMMAD DIED in A.D. 632. A century after his death his followers ruled over an empire extending across the whole of North Africa, across the straits and into Spain, as well as all the Middle East, and Asia to the borders of India and China. In all the African lands conquered by the Arabs Arabic to this day remains the dominant language; while the faith of Islam spread south across the desert to areas outside Arab rule. In the coastlands Islam almost completely obliterated all trace of previous religions or cultures. Ever since the conquest, and more than ever today, these have been Arab lands.

Far up the Nile valley, to the south of conquered Egypt, Ethiopia, isolated in her mountains, remained Christian.

MAP 10

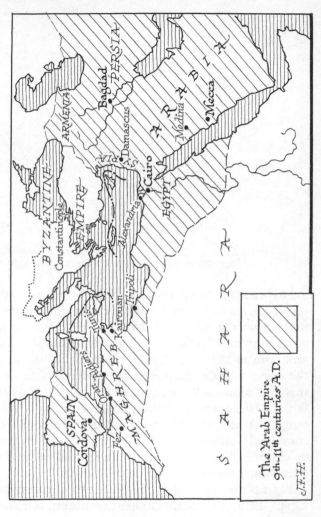

PERSIA

Bagdad

ARMENIA

ARABIA

Medina • Mecca

Damascus

BYZANTINE EMPIRE

Constantinople

Cairo

EGYPT

Alexandria

Tripoli

Kairouan

Tunis

MAGHREB

Oran-Algiers

Fez

SAHARA

SPAIN

Cordova

The Arab Empire.
9th–11th centuries A.D.

J.F.H.

THE ARAB EMPIRE

"FROM THEIR peninsula [Arabia]," writes Edward Atiyah,[1] "the Arabs brought two great contributions: Islam and the Arabic language, together with their code of desert chivalry. They also brought the psychological stimulus of their impact, as a vigorous conquering people, on the stagnant, if more civilised inhabitants of the outside world. In this world there was Greek philosophy, Roman ideas of law and government, Byzantine and Persian art, Christian theology and the Judaic tradition. Arab civilisation was a product of all these factors." In its golden age, from the 9th to the 11th century, there were two great centres west and east: Cordova, in Spain, and Bagdad, on the Tigris. During those two hundred years these two cities were perhaps the most important centres of world civilisation. When the Arab empire broke up, Tunis and Cairo were the capitals of kingdoms. Decay set in with the coming of the Ottoman Turks in the 14th-15th centuries. The countries of the Maghreb degenerated into pirate statelets, while Tripoli and Egypt were ruled (or misruled) by Turkish governors.

[1] *The Arabs.*

MAP 11

Trans-desert routes

Ceuta · Oran · Tunis
Fez · Tlemsen · Kairouan
Marrakesh · Tripoli
MOROCCO

S A H A R A

Ghat

HOGGAR

R. Senegal · Walata · Timbuktu · Agades
Ghana · SONGHAI · Gao
R. Gambia · GHANA · Mali · Djenne
S · MALI · U · Sokoto · BORNU
MOSSI · HAUSA Kingdoms · L. CHAD · to Egypt
Niger · R. Benue
R. Volta · BENIN
F O R E S T

J.F.H.

Area of Negro empires & kingdoms

40

KINGDOMS OF THE WESTERN SUDAN

SOUTH OF THE Sahara desert, stretching right across Africa from the Atlantic to the Red Sea, is a belt of savannah to which the Arabs gave the name of "Sudan." In the Niger region, in the western half of the Sudan, large, well-organised Negro states were established and flourished during the period called by Europeans the Middle Ages, some of them continuing down to the 19th century. They traded with the Arabs to the north, and Muslim learning and culture was diffused throughout a large part of the area. Timbuktu, on the middle Niger, was an important centre both of Islamism and of commerce.

The map shows only a few of the more outstanding of these kingdoms:—*Ghana* (5th-12th centuries) which lay far to the north of the present Ghana, between the Senegal and the middle Niger; *Mali*, which conquered Ghana, with an empire extending at one time from the Atlantic coast almost as far east as Lake Chad; the *Songhai* kingdom, with its capital at Gao, which was at the height of its power in the 16th century, stretching far north into the Sahara.

When these states declined power moved east to the Hausa kingdoms and Bornu. Later still the kingdoms of Ife and Benin flourished near the mouth of the Niger. By this time, of course, Europeans—Portuguese, British, French, Dutch—were establishing their trading stations along the coast, and the main trade routes were shifting from the Sahara to the Atlantic.

African nationalists today, proud of their history, are reviving the names of these past kingdoms (e.g. Ghana and Mali).

MAP 12

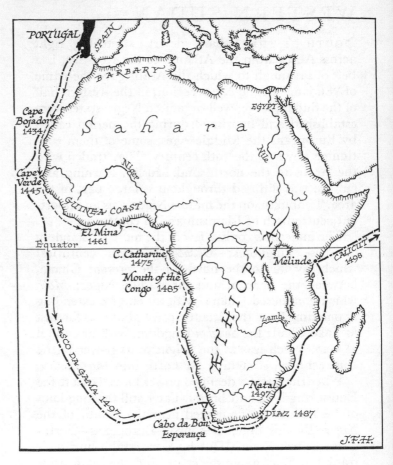

WESTERN EUROPE
RE-DISCOVERS AFRICA

POMPONIUS MELA, the Roman geographer (A.D. 50) who drew the map inset in No. 8, taught that the earth consisted of continents surrounded by water, and that India therefore could be reached by a sea passage round Africa. Prince Henry of Portugal, called "the Navigator," (1394-1463) believed that P. Mela was right, and sent out expeditions to sail down the African coast. He was also not averse to shipping some of the gold from the Guinea coast, news of which (*via* the Moors) had reached Western Europe. Expedition after expedition sailed. His sailors at first refused to go beyond Cape Bojador, being certain that God would turn them black if they went further. But the following year another ship sailed nearly 400 miles beyond Bojador without dire results.

Prince Henry died in 1463, but the voyages of discovery went on; and at last, in 1487, Bartolomeo Diaz rounded the Cape of Good Hope (having among his crew Columbus's brother). In 1493 Columbus (for Spain) discovered America. Six years later the King of Portugal ordered Vasco da Gama, with three ships, to sail round the Cape and go on to India. For the next three centuries Africa, south of the equator, was for Europeans no more than a coast-line, with ports of call, on the way to India.

MAP 13

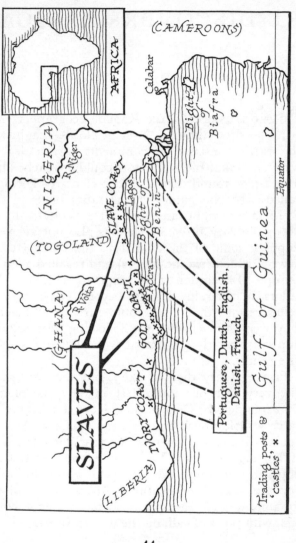

THE SLAVE TRADE

THE 16TH CENTURY opened the Atlantic chapter in European—and world—history. For the next 400 years the European countries facing the Atlantic Ocean were to take the lead in world affairs. The New World, on the western side of the ocean, went by the Pope's orders to Spain (Brazil excepted); Africa and Asia to Portugal. But England and France quickly challenged the Papal dispensation, both in North America and in Africa; and the two sides of the ocean were soon linked in a particularly dreadful way. I quote Norman Leys:[1] "The methods of exploitation followed by the Spaniards in America destroyed by the million the peoples they had conquered. But the exploitation was so profitable that the demand arose for workers who would last longer in slavery on plantations and in mines. That demand, reinforced a little later by Portuguese, French, English and Dutch officials and adventurers, was supplied by West Africa."

The slave trade went on for three centuries. It was perhaps the ghastliest crime (not forgetting Hitler) ever committed against a people. It made European merchants rich; and it provided the necessary labour-power for the economic development of South and southern North America.

[1] *Kenya*, p. 22.

45

MAP 14

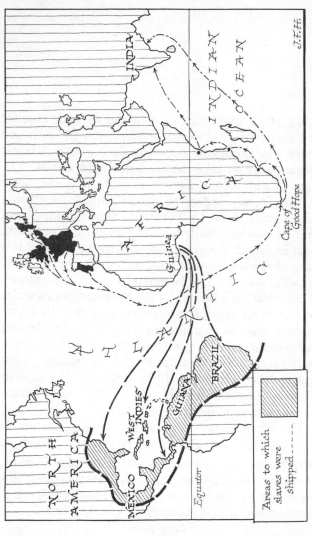

J.F.H.

INDIA

INDIAN OCEAN

Cape of Good Hope

AFRICA

Guinea

ATLANTIC

BRAZIL

GUIANA

WEST INDIES

NORTH AMERICA

MEXICO

Equator

Areas to which slaves were shipped------

46

"PIECES OF INDIA"

IN THE REIGN of Charles II this trading prospectus was issued in London:

> "The Spaniards treated with the Royal African Company of England for five thousand whole Pieces of India the Year, for 7 Years to be delivered at some of the Islands . . .
>
> A whole Piece of India was according to the Ages of the Negroes, Male or Female. Those between 15 and 45 were a whole Piece; between 4 and 8 were 2 for 1; between 8 and 15, or above 45, were 3 for 2, and those under 4 were cast in with the Mother.
>
> Such a Trade as this made by an Act of Parliament for 99 Years certain, would much improve all our Western Plantations, and by degrees perhaps find as good Mines in Carolina as in Potosi; 'twou'd increase Seamen and Ships for our use at home and encourage Growths and Manufactures here greatly; 'twill bring us in Gold apace to make Guineas with, and the Goods from the Plantations will fetch us in Silver, besides the Silver gotten for the Blacks. . . ."

At the lowest computation, says Norman Leys, 8 million Africans were sold in America, and at least five times as many persons perished in the slave raids and in the "middle passage"—the voyage across the Atlantic.

MAP 15

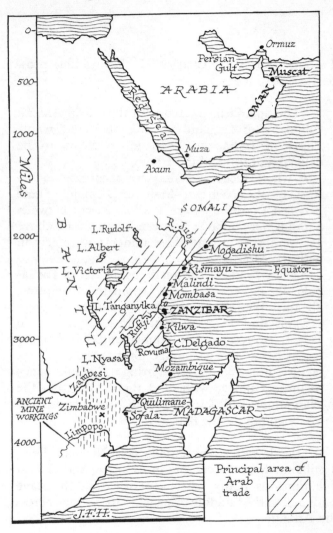

Ormuz

Persian
Gulf

ARABIA

Muscat

OMAN

Red Sea

Muza

Axum

SOMALI

R. Juba

L. Rudolf

L. Albert

Mogadishu

L. Victoria

Kismayu

Equator

Malindi

Mombasa

L. Tanganyika

ZANZIBAR

Rufiji

Kilwa

C. Delgado

L. Nyasa

Rovuma

Mozambique

Zambesi

MADAGASCAR

ANCIENT
MINE
WORKINGS

Zimbabwe

Quilimane

Sofala

Limpopo

Miles

0

500

1000

2000

3000

4000

Principal area of
Arab
trade

J.F.H.

THE EAST COAST

OVER ON THE the eastern side of Africa the Arabs had been trading and establishing coastal settlements since the 1st century A.D. According to the *Periplus of the Erythrean Sea*, written by an Egyptian Greek (A.D. 80), East Africa, under the rule of Arabs from Oman, was exporting ivory, rhinoceros horn, and (domestic) slaves. In the 12th century A.D. the Arab historian Edrisi records that the iron of Sofala (the southernmost name on our map) was much in demand by sword-makers in India.

When the Portuguese arrived in the early 16th century they conquered the whole coast from the Limpopo up to the "horn of Africa" (Somaliland). But their hold on the northern part crumbled as their Asiatic empire dwindled, and the Arabs came back into their own everywhere but in the region of Mozambique, which the Portuguese hold to this day (see Map 28). In the middle of the 19th century the Sultan of Oman transferred his "capital" to Zanzibar; and the trade in slaves was still continuing when Livingstone made his journeys of exploration (see next map).

MAP 16

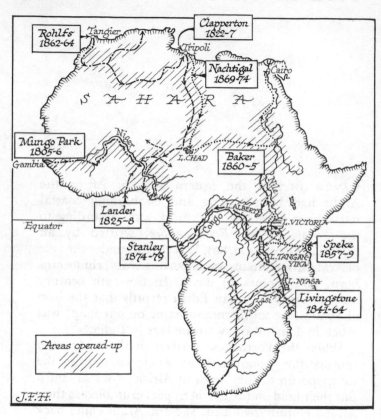

Rohlfs 1862-64

Tangier

Clapperton 1822-7

Tripoli

Nachtigal 1869-74

Cairo

S A H A R A

Mungo Park 1805-6

Niger

L. CHAD

Baker 1860-5

Gambia

Nile

Lander 1825-8

Equator

L. ALBERT

L. VICTORIA

Congo

Stanley 1874-79

L. TANGAN-YIKA

Speke 1857-9

L. NYASA

Zambesi

Livingstone 1841-64

Areas opened-up

J.F.H.

EXPLORERS AND MISSIONARIES

IN THE LAST quarter of the 18th century England (or some at least of the English) was beginning to be ashamed of its leading part in the slave trade. The abolitionists were making themselves heard, and a new and more civilised interest in Africa was developing. In 1788 the African Association was formed under the presidency of the scientist, Sir Joseph Banks, and in 1795 it sent out Mungo Park to solve the problem of the Niger. Ten years later Park made a second journey, at Government expense. He established the fact, unknown before, that the Niger flowed eastward. He sailed down the river for nearly two-thirds of its length before he was killed (1806).

From then onwards, for three-quarters of the century, explorers—British, French and German— "opened up" the interior of the Unknown Continent the Sahara, the sources of the Nile, the Congo and Zambesi regions. Some of them were missionaries, some government emissaries. The later explorations, like Stanley's in the Congo region, paved the way for the partition of Africa among the Western European countries.

Some part of Europe's debt to Africa was, and is being, paid by the Christian missions. Until recently they were responsible for whatever educational work was being done; and if many missionaries were narrowly unsympathetic to African culture and ideology, many also were—and are—courageous defenders of the African against exploitation of various kinds.

MAP 17

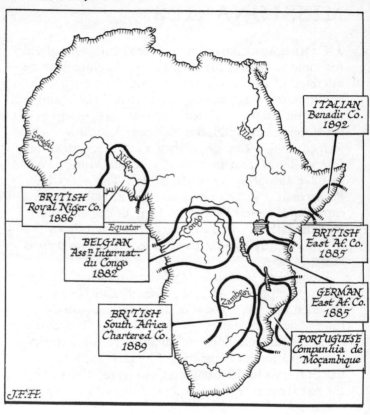

ITALIAN
Benadir Co.
1892

Senegal

Nile

Niger

BRITISH
Royal Niger Co.
1886

Equator

BELGIAN
Ass.ⁿ Internat.
du Congo
1882

Congo

BRITISH
East Af. Co.
1885

GERMAN
East Af. Co.
1885

Zambesi

BRITISH
South Africa
Chartered Co.
1889

PORTUGUESE
Companhia de
Moçambique

J.F.H.

THE CHARTERED
COMPANIES

WE HAVE NOW reached the period of the Great Scramble—turn back to Maps 1 and 2.

Having drawn straight lines[1] in all directions across the map of Africa and parcelled out the continent between them, the European governments gave to Chartered Companies the job (and the profits) of "developing" the hundreds of thousands of square miles of new territory. These Companies were given monopoly rights of exploitation in their respective areas. After a time they were usually bought out, and the territories formally annexed, or placed under "protection." The British operated west, south, and east (see map). King Leopold of the Belgians' Association Internationale du Congo had the centre of the continent. Karl Peters' German East Africa Company, the Portuguese Companhia de Moçambique, and the Italian Benadir Company took areas on the east coast. French trading companies, dating from the 18th century, were still operating from the Senegal region in the north-west.

[1] It should be noted that these straight lines resulted in purely artificial frontiers, which often cut tribes and peoples in two. Now that Africans are claiming the right to govern themselves some re-alignment of frontiers is often essential.

MAP 18

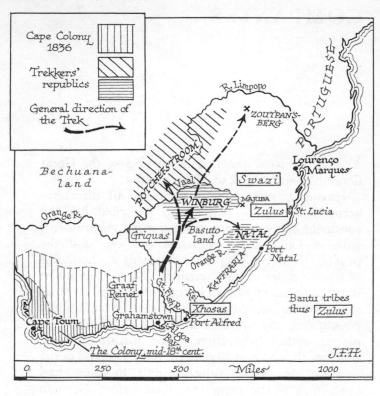

Cape Colony 1836

Trekkers' republics

General direction of the Trek

Bechuana-land

R. Limpopo

× ZOUTPANS-BERG

PORTUGUESE

Lourenço Marques

Swazi

POTCHEFSTROOM

Vaal

WINBURG

MAJUBA ×

Zulus St. Lucia

Orange R.

Griquas

Basuto-land

NATAL

Orange R.

Port Natal

KAFFRARIA

Graaf Reinet

Gt. Fish R.

Rei

Bantu tribes thus Zulus

Cape Town

Grahamstown

Algoa Bay

Xhosas

Port Alfred

The Colony, mid-18th cent.

J.F.H.

0   250   500   Miles   1000

THE DUTCH TREK NORTH

MORE THAN a century before the British South Africa Chartered Company commenced operations Dutch and British were established in a small colony in the extreme south of the continent, at the Cape. (The Dutchman Van Riebeck had landed with a handful of Dutch and Swedish settlers as far back as 1652, when the Cape was a "cabbage-garden" for the supply of fresh vegetables on the route to India.) The colony changed hands between British and Dutch once or twice during the Napoleonic wars. In 1820 a body of some 5000 English settlers arrived. Fourteen years later, groups of Dutch farmers (Boers), impatient at the more humane British attitude to the natives, trekked north and founded the independent republics of Potchefstroom (later the Transvaal), Winburg (Orange Free State), and Natal. The last-named lasted only ten years, the British annexing it in 1843. The Boer advance was fiercely contested by the Africans—Xhosas, Zulus, Swazis.

In 1877 the two Boer republics were re-annexed to Britain, but only four years later regained their independence after defeating a British force at Majuba Hill.

MAP 19

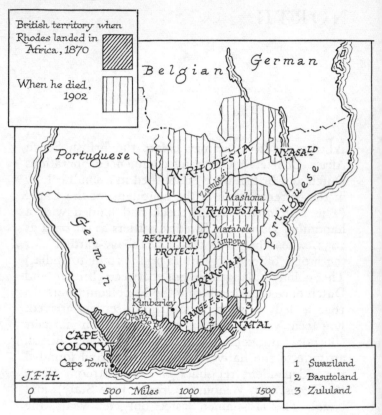

British territory when
Rhodes landed in
Africa, 1870

When he died,
1902

Belgian

German

Portuguese

N. RHODESIA

NYASA LD

Zambesi

Mashona

S. RHODESIA

German

BECHUANA LD
PROTECT.

Matabele

Limpopo

TRANSVAAL

Portuguese

Kimberley

ORANGE F.S.

1

3

CAPE
COLONY

Orange R.

2

NATAL

Cape Town

J.F.H.

0   500   Miles   1000   1500

1 Swaziland
2 Basutoland
3 Zululand

56

DIAMONDS AND GOLD

In 1870 a Boer farmer found his children playing with a bright stone. He took it to a nearby town and sold it for £500. A rush of diamond diggers began, and the area (Kimberley) was promptly annexed by Britain. Cecil Rhodes' elder brother was among the first prospectors, and Cecil shortly joined him.

In an amazingly short time he was a wealthy man. He did no more digging, concentrating on big business combinations and trusts. De Beers Consolidated Mines had a monopoly of South African diamonds—90% of the world supply. Then gold was discovered on the Rand, in the Transvaal, and Rhodes founded Goldfields of South Africa, Ltd. He went into politics and became Prime Minister of the Cape Colony. His South Africa Chartered Company, after wars with Matabele and Mashonas, secured control of vast areas to the north—Bechuanaland (a protectorate) and the lands north and south of the Zambesi, named after him the Rhodesias.

The map shows the growth of British-controlled territory in South Africa during his lifetime.

MAP 20

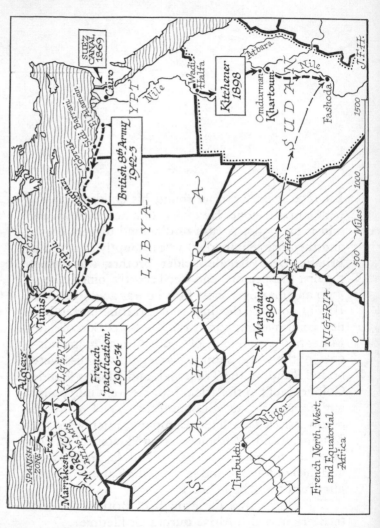

WARS AND "PACIFICA-TIONS" IN THE NORTH

THE MAP COVERS the events of half-a-century in the north of the continent.

In 1885 a religious revolt in the Egyptian Sudan, led by the Mahdi, led to the siege and capture of Khartoum and the killing of General Gordon, head of a British-Egyptian force sent south from British-occupied Egypt (the Suez Canal had been opened in 1869). In 1898 a British-Egyptian army under Kitchener defeated the Khalifa, the Mahdi's successor, at Omdurman, so securing the Sudan for Britain.

A French force under Captain Marchand had been marching eastward through the French Sudan, but reached Fashoda, on the Nile, only to find the Union Jack flying. French Africa was *not* to extend across the continent from west to east.

In 1904 Britain agreed to France having a free hand in Morocco in return for French acquiescence in the British control of Egypt. For nearly 30 years the French were engaged in the "pacification" (i.e. conquest) of Morocco, under the command of the great soldier-administrator, Lyautey.

During the Second World War, after a German-Italian army under Rommel had pushed over the Libyan frontier into Egypt, the British Eighth Army under Montgomery advanced from El Alamein along the thousand miles across Libya to Tunis.

MAP 21

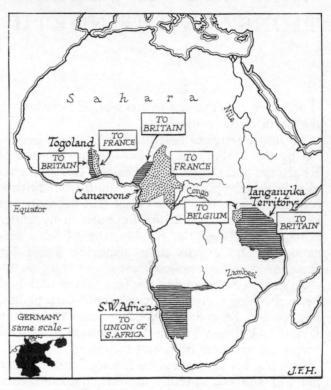

THE FIRST EUROPEAN EMPIRE LIQUIDATED

THE PEACE settlement after the First World War ended the German empire in Africa, the German colonies being handed over as "mandates" to other Powers. Togoland and the Cameroons were divided between Britain and France; German East Africa was taken over by Britain as Tanganyika Territory (self-government, 1960); a small eastern part of it, Ruanda-Urundi, went to the Belgian Congo; German South-West Africa to the Union of South Africa.

After the Second World War the Union of South Africa declined to make any trusteeship agreement with the United Nations, and has administered the territory as a part of the Union. Native lands have been expropriated for the benefit of white settlers, and the chiefs of the Herero tribe were prevented from leaving Africa to present their protest to the United Nations. Their case was taken up and their cause pleaded by the Rev. Michael Scott. Seventy per cent of the *voters* in the territory are Afrikaners, twenty-two per cent speak German, and the remainder English.

MAP 22

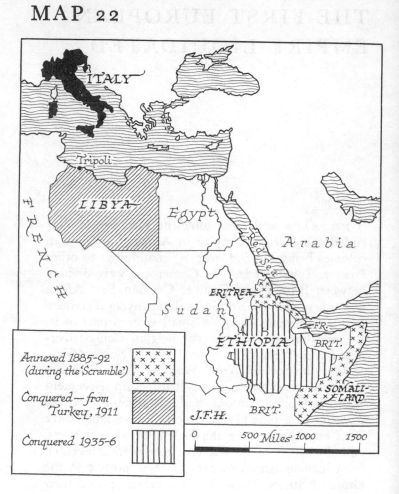

ITALY

Tripoli

LIBYA

Egypt

Arabia

Red Sea

FRENCH

Sudan

ERITREA

FR.

ETHIOPIA

BRIT.

SOMALI-LAND

Annexed 1885-92
(during the 'Scramble')

Conquered — from
Turkey, 1911

Conquered 1935-6

J.F.H.

BRIT.

0   500 Miles 1000   1500

—AND THE SECOND

ITALY'S EMPIRE in Africa consisted of Eritrea and Somaliland, north and south-east respectively of Ethiopia (Abyssinia); and Libya, conquered from Turkey in 1911-12. An Italian invasion of Abyssinia in 1896 came to a disastrous conclusion at Adowa. Mussolini avenged this defeat by the successful war of 1935. But at the end of the Second World War Ethiopia regained its independence, and Eritrea became an autonomous province under Ethiopian suzerainty. Italian Somaliland became Somalia, a trusteeship territory under Italian administration until December, 1960, when it will become an independent sovereign state—probably linked with British Somaliland.

Libya became independent in 1951.

PART II
TODAY

MAP 23

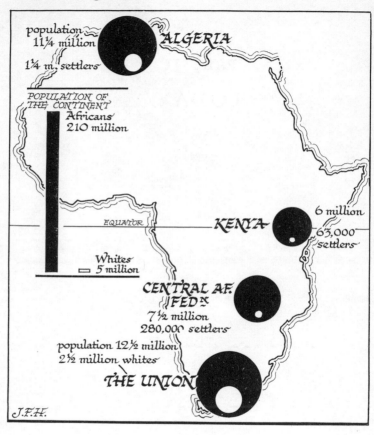

population 11¼ million
1¼ m. settlers

ALGERIA

POPULATION OF
THE CONTINENT
Africans
210 million

EQUATOR

KENYA

6 million
63,000 settlers

Whites
5 million

CENTRAL AF.
FED.ⁿ
7½ million
280,000 settlers

population 12½ million
2½ million whites

THE UNION

J.F.H.

THE TROUBLE SPOTS

The four black blots—one should rather say white blots—on the map of Africa, the territories which keep Africa on the front page of the newspapers, are the four areas in which there has been considerable white settlement. In Kenya and the Union there has also been a considerable influx of Asians, chiefly Indians. The problem in each case, therefore, is to find a satisfactory "balance of power" between racial groups differing widely in social and educational development.

The French connection with *Algeria* dates from 1830 (well before the Scramble) when a French fleet bombarded and occupied Algiers, the capital city of a sultanate notorious for piracy. Despite repeated Arab revolts settlement in the fertile coastal belt by Italians as well as French steadily increased. Tension has been growing ever since the Second World War, and has resulted during the past few years in a bitter guerilla war in which very large French forces have been engaged.

For the *Union of South Africa* see Maps 34 and 35.

In *Kenya* and the *Rhodesias (Central African Federation)* white settlement began only in the present century; in the former, after the construction of a railway from the coast to Uganda had shown that the Kenyan highlands, though so close to the equator, had a climate suited to Europeans; in the Rhodesias, after Cecil Rhodes' Chartered Company had opened up the central areas to the Zambesi and beyond (cf. Map 17).

MAP 24

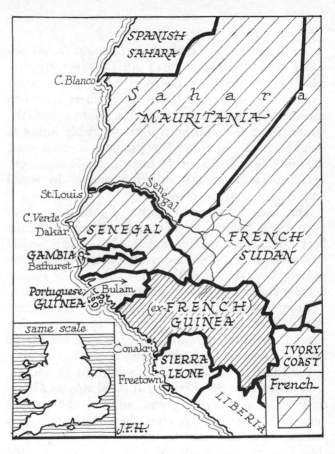

WEST COAST BEGINNINGS

THE RELATIVELY small colonies on the northwest coast of the continent mostly dated from the days before the Great Scramble.

Spanish Sahara (Rio de Oro) is mainly desert, with a sparse population of nomad Arabs.

Mauritania (now an Islamic Republic) and *Senegal*, whose capital, Dakar, was formerly the administrative centre of all French West Africa, are now both autonomous republics of the French Community. Senegal is now amalgamated with *Sudan* in the *Mali Federation*. *Guinea* was the only territory to opt for complete independence from France in the de Gaulle referendum of 1948. (For these French areas see also Maps 30 and 31.)

The small British colony of the *Gambia* is likely, it is reported, to be amalgamated with the Mali Federation soon. To judge from its size and position on the map this would be sensible. *Sierra Leone* was originally an asylum for Africans rescued from slave-ships by the British when abolition was being enforced.

Portuguese Guinea was founded 500 years ago, soon after Prince Henry's seamen made their first voyages down the African coast (cf. Map 12).

For *Liberia* see Map 38.

MAP 25

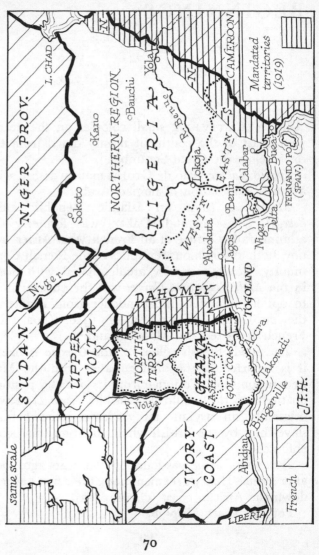

L. CHAD

NIGER PROV.

NORTHERN REGION
o Kano
Sokoto
o Bauchi

NIGERIA
Yola

R. Benue

N

CAMEROON

Mandated territories (1919)

Lokoja
EAST'N
Calabar
Benin
Abeokuta
WEST'N
Lagos
Buea
FERNANDO PO (SPAN.)
Niger Delta

SUDAN

Niger

DAHOMEY

TOGOLAND

UPPER VOLTA

NORTHN TERR.s
GHANA
ASHANTI
GOLD COAST
Accra
Takoradi
Bingerville

R. Volta

IVORY COAST

Abidjan

LIBERIA

J.F.H.

same scale

French

70

WEST COAST *(continued)*

In March, 1957, the colony of the Gold Coast became the first British African territory to become an independent state. It called itself *Ghana*, from the ancient Negro Kingdom of that name (see Map 11). It exports cocoa (70% of the total value of exports), gold, bauxite, timber and diamonds, through two deep-water ports, Takoradi and Tema. The Volta River Project, to be administered on the lines of the T.V.A. in the United States, would generate electricity, supply water for irrigation, and exploit the large deposits of bauxite and aluminium.

In 1960 the Federation of *Nigeria* (population 32 million) also becomes independent. Its three regions —*Northern, Western* and *Eastern* (capitals, Kaduna, Ibadan and Enugu)—each have their own governments. Agriculture produces 90% of Nigeria's exports and occupies 80% of its working population. But it exports 5% of the world's tin, and oilfields in Eastern Nigeria, with a pipeline to Port Harcourt, are now being developed. After Egypt, Nigeria (see Map 42) is the area of densest population in Africa.

The western part of the trust territory of *Togoland* was joined to Ghana in 1956. The eastern part is now an independent republic. The two areas of *Northern* and *Southern Cameroons* which had been administered, under trust, as parts of Nigeria, are to decide whether to continue the Nigerian connection, to join the Cameroons, or to become independent.

For the French territories see Map 31.

MAP 26

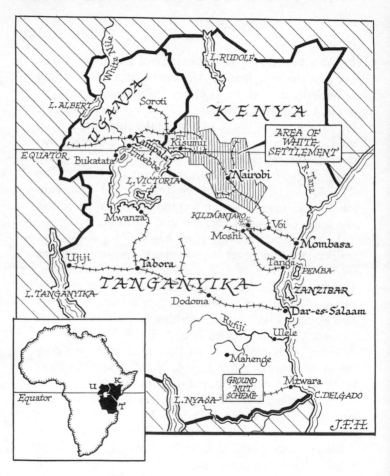

EAST COAST (BRITISH)

KENYA, *Uganda*, *Tanganyika* and *Zanzibar*, the four British-controlled territories in East Africa, make up an area nearly a quarter the size of the U.S.A., with a total population of 21 million.

For centuries the coast towns were under Arab dominance (see Map 15), and the interior—of Tanganyika particularly—was a raiding ground for Arab slavers.

The opening-up of *Kenya* by the building of the railway to Kampala, in *Uganda*, has already been mentioned (Map 23). The Africans were moved into reserves—Kikuyu reserve, density 283 per square mile; Kavirondo, 145. "Unrest" reached a climax in the Kikuyu "Mau Mau" rebellion in 1952-3. The White Highlands have now been opened to non-Europeans, and a new constitution (1960) has greatly increased African participation in the Government.

Tanganyika, formerly German East Africa, was administered under mandate, 1919-60, but is to achieve independent self-government this year.

Zanzibar, an Arab sultanate, came under British protection soon after the British East Africa Company was established (see Map 17).

Uganda was included in the British sphere at the same time. Recent developments there have centred on a three-cornered struggle between the British Government, a feudal autocrat (the Kabaka of the Buganda, whose realm forms part of the country) and the African nationalists demanding the end both of black feudalism and white imperialism.

73

MAP 27

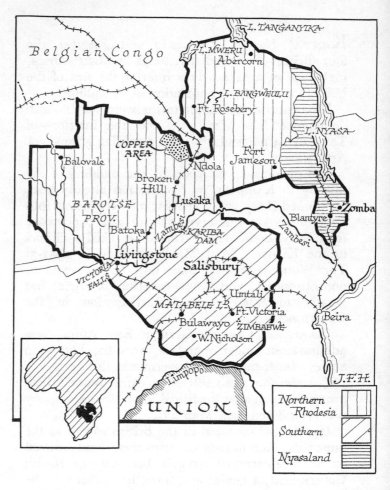

Belgian Congo

L. TANGANYKA

L. MWERU
Abercorn

L. BANGWEULU

Ft. Rosebery

L. NYASA

COPPER
AREA

Balovale

Ndola

Fort
Jameson

Broken
Hill

*BAROTSE
PROV.*

Lusaka

Batoka

Zambesi

*KARIBA
DAM*

Blantyre

Zambesi

Zomba

Livingstone

*VICTORIA
FALLS*

Salisbury

Umtali

MATABELE L

Ft. Victoria

Bulawayo

ZIMBABWE

Beira

W. Nicholson

Limpopo

UNION

J.F.H.

| Northern Rhodesia |
| Southern |
| Nyasaland |

74

FROM RHODES TO WELENSKY

THE TWO *Rhodesias*, Northern and Southern, and *Nyasaland* were joined to form the *Central African Federation* in 1953. The Rhodesias were a British heritage from the days of Cecil Rhodes (see Map 19), Nyasaland from the days of a very different man, David Livingstone. (But it was not until 1891 that Nyasaland, largely as a result of missionary effort by the Church of Scotland, asked for British protection.) Though by far the smallest of the three territories, Nyasaland has the largest population.

The native policy of the C.A.F. is allegedly based on "partnership" of whites and Africans; but it is clearly a partnership of first- and second-class citizens. From the African point of view Sir Roy Welensky's policy of "parallel development" is barely distinguishable from the Union of South Africa's *apartheid*. Nyasaland has from the outset been strongly opposed to federation. Disturbances in 1959 resulted in the declaration of a state of emergency, and the detention of Dr. Banda and other African leaders. In 1960 the British Government appointed a Commission, under the chairmanship of Lord Monckton, to report on the situation.

The most important economic asset of the area is the copper field of N. Rhodesia, the third largest in the world.

MAP 28

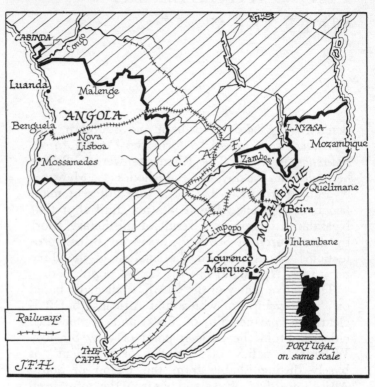

CABINDA

Luanda

Malenge

ANGOLA

Benguela

Nova
Lisboa

Mossamedes

Congo

C. A. E.

Zambesi

L.NYASA

Mozambique

MOZAMBIQUE

Quelimane

Beira

Limpopo

Inhambane

Lourenço
Marques

Railways
+++++

THE
CAPE

J.F.H.

PORTUGAL
on same scale

PORTUGAL IN AFRICA

BESIDES *Portuguese Guinea* (see Map 24) Portugal
still holds two areas of considerable size on the west
and east coasts of Africa respectively—*Angola* and
Mozambique. They are probably the most backward
areas of the whole continent, though they are undoubtedly paying propositions economically.

They are governed directly by the dictatorship
which rules Portugal itself as "Overseas Provinces"
of the metropolitan country, and the political rights
of all inhabitants, black or white, are rigidly limited.
On the other hand, there is practically no colour
bar. The races mix freely, and even inter-marry;
and Africans who pass certain tests can qualify for
such civilised rights as exist, being then known as
assimilados. This probably accounts for the absence,
up to now, of an African nationalist movement.
(The "primitives", however, vastly out-number the
assimilados.)

The Benguela railway, running east across Angola,
links up with the central Cape-Congo line, and
thence to Beira, in Mozambique, thus completing
the only west-east rail communication across the
continent.

MAP 29

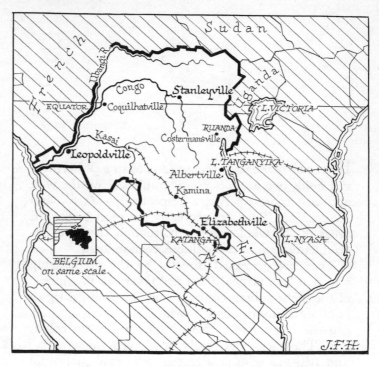

KING LEOPOLD'S CRUSADE

In 1 8 7 6 King Leopold of the Belgians summoned a "geographic conference" to Brussels, and made a speech in which he said—"To open to civilisation the only area where it has not yet penetrated, to pierce the darkness which envelops whole populations, is a crusade . . . worthy of this century of progress." A "Committee for the Study of the Upper Congo" was formed, and H. M. Stanley sent to Africa to carry out studies on the spot. In 1885 the Congo "Free" State was inaugurated, with Leopold as its sovereign. One of the concessionaire companies made a net profit in six years of over 3 million dollars on a paid-up capital of 45,000.[1] A few years later the world shuddered when Roger Casement's investigations found that the people of the Congo were being treated "with inconceivable brutality", and E. D. Morel, in *Red Rubber*, published the facts.

In 1908 the Free State became a Belgian colony, and a "paternalist" native policy was adopted. A sudden—and to outsiders unexpected—outbreak of nationalist and inter-tribal revolt occurred in 1959; and the Belgian Government without delay acceded to African demands, independence being promised for June, 1960. The colony, it seems, had become too great a burden on the Belgian tax-payer.

Disorders in Ruanda-Urundi; the small area held by Belgium under trust (see Map 21) led to a United Nations recommendation that it should be granted separate independence.

[1] P. T. Moon, *Imperialism and World Politics*, p. 87.

MAP 30

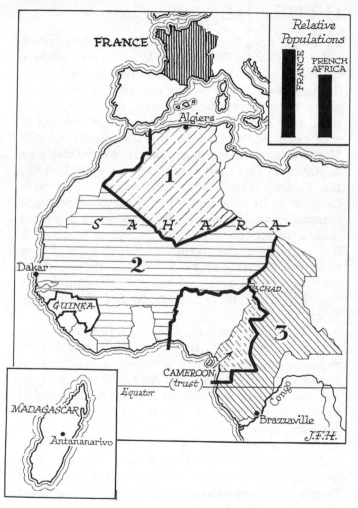

FRANCE IN AFRICA

FRENCH AFRICA (exclusive of Madagascar) covered a huge area of some 4 million square miles —nearly twice as large as the U.S.A. Most of the colonies which it comprised are now, by their own choice, "autonomous republics within the French Community".

The three main zones are: (1) *French North Africa*, now, after the winning of complete independence by Morocco and Tunisia, reduced to Algeria (see Maps 32 and 33); (2) *French West Africa* (see following map for the various component territories); (3) *French Equatorial Africa*, extending from the Sahara to south of the Congo.

The links between metropolitan France and these colonies have been close—and material. "The French tax-payer in the last 10 years has provided about five times more for the French African territories than the British tax-payer has provided for British Africa with twice the population"·[1] a fact which doubtless had something to do with the decision of so many of the colonies to remain within the Community. Indeed, Dr. Houphouet-Boigny, leader of the largest nationalist movement in French Africa, has said: "If we had been colonised by the British we should no doubt have opted for independence".

The island of *Madagascar* (population 5 million) has been French—after a bombardment of the capital—since 1896. It is to become independent this year (1960).

[1] J. H. Huizinga (*African Affairs*, January, 1959)

MAP 31

Independent

Federation of Mali

FRANCE

Algiers

ALGERIA
part of Metropolitan
France

MAURITANIA

SUDAN

NIGER

CHAD

Dakar

SENEGAL

GAMBIA

GUINEA

UBANGI-CHARI

CAMEROON

HIGH VOLTA

DAHOMEY

IVORY COAST

TOGOLAND

GABON

EQUATOR

(GHANA)

Brazzaville

J.F.H.

MIDDLE CONGO

FRANCE IN AFRICA
(continued)

THE ONLY French territory to declare for sovereign independence in the 1958 referendum was *Guinea* (population 2½ million). France's retort was so complete a withdrawal of men and equipment as to make the future of the new state highly uncertain. Ghana's offer of a close union and a loan of £10 million saved the situation. (A not inconsiderable obstacle to the union is that the Prime Ministers of the two states can talk only through an interpreter; President Touré speaks only French, Dr. Nkrumah only English—they have no common African language.

For *Togoland* and the *Cameroons* see Map 25.

Will the various autonomous republics remain separate or will they federate—in one body, or in groups? *Senegal* and *Sudan* have already formed the Federation of *Mali* (another name revived from pre-European Africa—see Map 11). It will attain full independence in 1960. The four equatorial territories (*Chad*, *Ubangi-Chari*—now called the *Central African Republic,*—*Gabon,* and *Middle Congo*—now the *Republic of the Congo*) have formed a customs and economic union.

Another question which only time can answer is—will the right-wing French National Assembly really acquiesce in treating these ex-colonies as real equals in the French Comminity? And if not, will there be more declarations of independence?

83

MAP 32

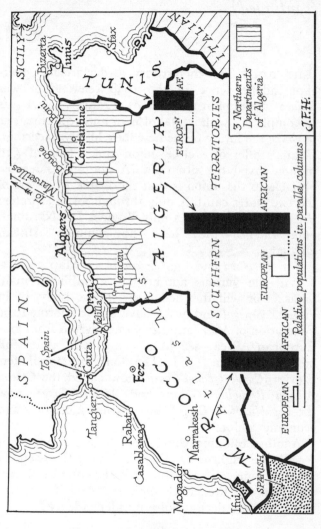

THE ARABS MAKE WAR

AT THE All-Africa Congress in Accra, December, 1958, the Algerian delegation succeeded in carrying an amendment to the platform resolution urging the attainment of independence by peaceful, constitutional methods. Where violence is used against a nationalist movement, said the Algerians, Africans must give their support to violent resistance.

For more than four years the bloody struggle has gone on in *Algeria*; and *Morocco* and *Tunis*, which won their independence from France in 1956, are torn between sympathy for their Algerian brethren and their desperate need to retain their economic links with France. In Tunisia, it is estimated a tenth of the population is unemployed. Yet Tunis cannot avoid establishing supply depots for the Algerian rebels along its frontiers—which does not increase French friendship. In Morocco, King Mohammed V faces leftist nationalist movements anxious to end his pro-Western policies, and to turn the U.S. out of its Moroccan naval and air bases.

Meantime the French settlers—the *colons*—of Algeria set their faces against any concessions by de Gaulle to the rebels, preferring, it would seem, to bring down the Fifth Republic.

MAP 33

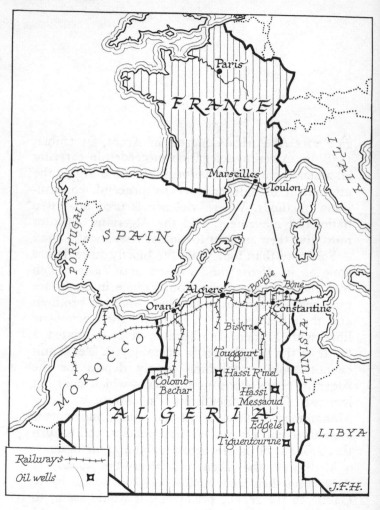

ALGERIA—EUROPEAN OR AFRICAN?

ALGERIA WAS THE first of the North African countries to be occupied by the French (1842), but it was many years before Arab resistance was overcome. "This resistance," Edward Atiyah points out,[1] "was the first reaction (a century ago) of the western Arab world to European imperialism." It is a grim coincidence that French Resistance to the German occupation of France stood up heroically to torture; and that Arab Resistance to the French occupation of Algeria has faced the same treatment.

The French, of course, now insist that Algeria is an integral part of metropolitan France; which means that the Arabs, in a large majority in Algeria, would be a permanent minority in France-cum-Algeria. President de Gaulle has made various speeches which can be interpreted either way.

The discovery of oil in the Sahara has naturally not made France any more anxious to hand over Algeria to the Algerians. The four-year war in Algeria has been as a matter of fact the biggest overseas military effort ever made by France. A Five Year Plan (economic and political) for Algeria, the "Constantine Programme," was announced by General de Gaulle in October, 1958. An Algerian "government-in-exile" is established at Cairo.

[1] *The Arabs*, p. 139.

MAP 34

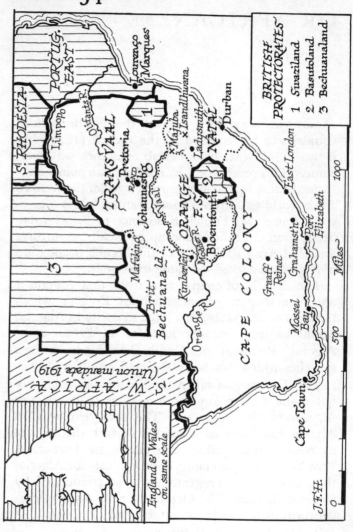

BRITISH PROTECTORATES

1 Swaziland
2 Basutoland
3 Bechuanaland

S. RHODESIA

PORTUG. EAST

Lourenço Marques

Limpopo R.

Olifants R.

TRANSVAAL

Pretoria

RAND

Johannesburg

x Majuba

x Isandlhwana

Ladysmith

Durban

NATAL

Vaal R.

ORANGE F.S.

Mafeking

Brit. Bechuana ld.

Kimberley

Modder R.

Bloemfontein

Orange R.

East London

Port Elizabeth

Graaff Reinet

Grahamstn

Mossel Bay

CAPE COLONY

Cape Town

S.W. AFRICA
(Union mandate 1919)

England & Wales on same scale

J.F.H.

Miles

0   500   1000

88

THE HOME OF APARTHEID

THE EVENTS of March-April, 1960, have made the whole world conscious of the Problem of South Africa. The British Liberal Government's decision (1909) to hand South Africa back to the Boers was hailed as a piece of generous and constructive statesmanship towards a defeated enemy. But, says Leonard Barnes,[1] "in doing a good turn to the Boers that Government did a very bad one to the much more numerous but defenceless natives. . . . As it happened there was a native population three times as large as Boers and Britons put together. . . . By its gesture of magnaminity towards the Boers, the Liberal Government virtually washed its hands of this [native] difficulty."

The South African Nationalist Party (in power since 1948) stands for the old Boer doctrine of White Supremacy. Its native policy is expressed in one word—*Apartheid*: segregation of blacks from whites, with all power, prestige, profit and political rights to the latter. It is a crazy doctrine, of course, as well as an immoral and un-Christian one—South Africa cannot develop as a modern industrial state without African labour.

The Union would like to absorb the three British Protectorates, two of them, *Swaziland* and *Basutoland*, within its borders. So far, no British Government has stooped so low as to consider handing them over.

[1] *The New Boer War.*

MAP 35

Nationalist Party
United Party
Doubtful

S. RHODESIA

Bechuanaland Protect.

S.W. AFRICA

TRANSVAAL
Pretoria
Mafeking
Johannesbg
Vereeniging
ORANGE F.S.
Kimberley
NATAL
Durban

1
2

1-Swaziland
2-Basutoland

C A P E

Cape Town
Port Elizabeth
East London

J.F.H.

90

THE POLITICS OF INEQUALITY

THE STRENGTH AND extent of the Nationalist Party in the Union of South Africa is illustrated by this map (copied, by permission, from *The Politics of Inequality*, by Gwen M. Carter). It is based on the results of the General Election of April, 1953. The United Party (the official Opposition) is practically confined, it will be noted, to the eastern end of the Cape Province and the old British colony of Natal, with smaller areas near Cape Town and Johannesburg.

The United Party does not oppose Apartheid—only some of the means used or proposed for carrying it into effect. A small break-away group, the Progressives, is more "moderate"; and there is a still smaller Liberal Party, with—so far—no parliamentary representation.

MAP 36

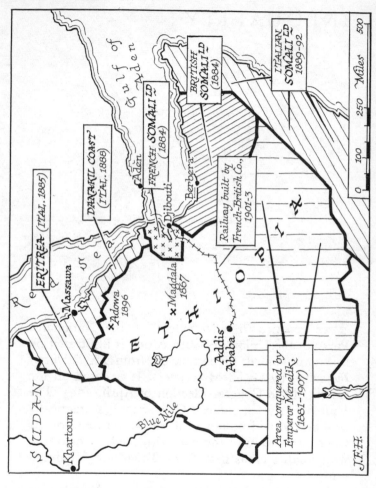

ERITREA (ITAL. 1885)

DANAKIL COAST (ITAL. 1888)

FRENCH SOMALILD (1884)

BRITISH SOMALILD (1884)

ITALIAN SOMALILD 1889-92

Railway built by French-British Co., 1901-3

Area conquered by Emperor Menelik (1881-1907)

Gulf of Aden

Aden

Djibouti

Berbera

E T H I O P I A

Massawa

×Adowa 1896

×Magdala 1867

Addis Ababa

Red Sea

S U D A N

Khartoum

Blue Nile

0   100   250   500   Miles

J.F.H.

MOUNTAIN KINGDOM

Except for the six years of the Italian occupation (1935-41) *Ethiopia* (Abyssinia) has kept its independence throughout the centuries of recorded African history.

It was invaded by the British, and its ruler defeated at Magdala, in 1867; and by the Italians, whom it heavily defeated at Adowa, in 1896. The same two Powers, *plus* France, snatched the coastlands all round it during the Great Scramble. Its ruler at this time, the Emperor Menelik, did some conquering on his own account, annexing large areas to the south of his original territory. It was in the latter years of his reign that a railway was built, linking his capital, Addis Ababa, to the coast at the French port of Djibouti.

By U.N. resolution the former Italian colony of *Eritrea* was federated (1952) with Ethiopia, which thus at last gained direct access to the sea.

MAP 37

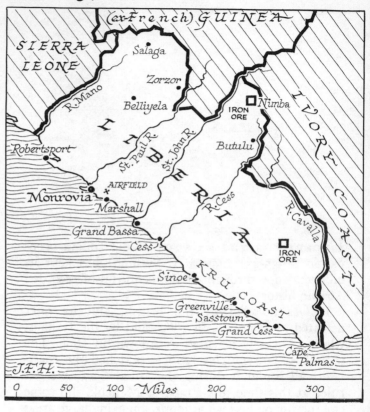

SIERRA LEONE

(ex French) GUINEA

Salaga

Zorzor

R.Mano

Belliyela

IVORY COAST

IRON ORE

Nimba

Robertsport

St.Paul R.

St.John R.

Butulu

LIBERIA

AIRFIELD

Monrovia

Marshall

R.Cess

R.Cavalla

Grand Bassa

IRON ORE

Cess

Sinoe

KRU COAST

Greenville

Sasstown

Grand Cess

Cape Palmas

J.F.H.

0   50   100   Miles   200   300

U.S.-ADOPTED

ONE SMALL INDEPENDENT African state has been in existence on the West Coast for over a century—*Liberia*. The American Government was finding the numbers of freed slaves an embarrassment, so a piece of territory adjoining Sierra Leone (also a home for freed slaves) was purchased, and the first batch of American negroes settled there, in 1822. The original area has been considerably increased since, and the tribes of the interior brought under the rule of their "Europeanised" brethren on the coast. Large road-building schemes have recently been inaugurated.

The (American) Firestone Company and the Goodrich Co. have extensive rubber plantations, and American, German, and Swedish-American companies are developing big iron-ore projects. The U.S. dollar is the medium of exchange.

The Heads of Government of Liberia, Ghana, and Guinea—President Tubman, Dr. Nkrumah, and M. Sekou Touré—have met in conference and discussed a "Community of African States"

MAP 38

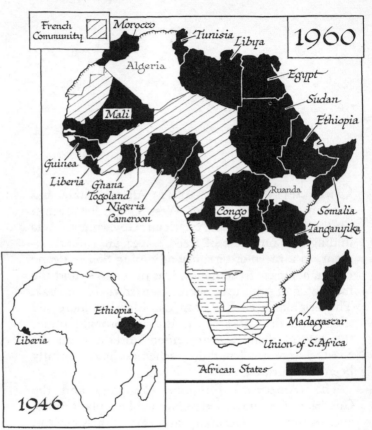

NEW STATES

EVENTS ARE moving so rapidly in Africa that by the time this map is in print the reader will probably have to make additions to it for himself.

It shows those African ex-colonies or protectorates which have become, or are on the verge of becoming, independent sovereign states. The member-republics of the French Community are not—yet—fully independent; and the Union of South Africa is not, of course, a free *African* state.

MAP 39

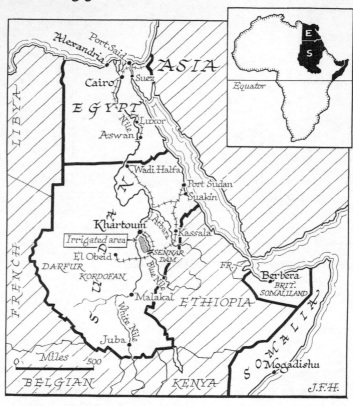

THE COUNTRIES OF
THE NILE

EGYPT, UNDER British administration from 1882 (from 1914 to 1922 it was a British Protectorate) became independent in 1936, but Britain still kept the right to maintain a garrison on the Suez Canal. In 1956, on the accession to the Presidency of Colonel Gamal Nasser, that garrison was withdrawn. Later that year, after Nasser had without warning nationalised the Canal, Britain, France and Israel invaded Egypt, but in deference to world opinion ceased hostilities in a few days. The "Suez Incident" undoubtedly strengthened Colonel Nasser's position as leader of the Arab world against the West.

The Sudan, before it attained full independence in 1956 had been an Anglo-Egyptian Condominium since 1899. Colonel Nasser's attempts to persuade it to accept some form of closer union with Egypt have so far failed. The key fact in Sudanese politics is the division of the country between an Arab-speaking Moslem north and a non-Moslem Negro south. The great achievement of British rule was the construction of the Sennar and Jebel Aulia dams, and the establishment of the highly successful co-operative cotton-growing enterprise—the Gezira Scheme; described as "one of the most interesting social, political and economic experiments outside the Soviet Union," representing "a very advanced stage of socialised farming." In January, 1959, a military coup by General Abboud abolished Parliament and all political parties, and put the Army in control.

MAP 40

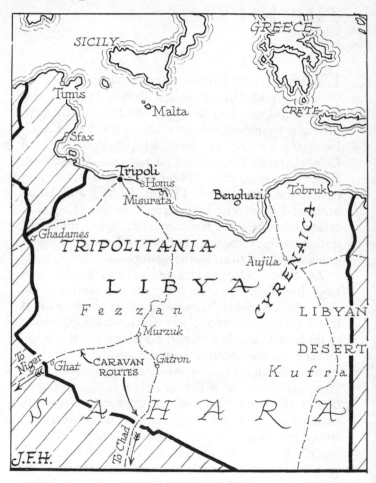

DESERT COUNTRY

LIBYA, WITH AN area larger than France, Italy, Britain, Spain and Germany combined (or three times the size of Texas) has a population of a little over a million. The country is mainly rock and sand desert, the few towns lying along the fertile coast strip. From the 16th century Libya was under Turkish rule, until, a couple of years before the First World War, Italy seized it, and proceeded to put a good deal of road construction in hand. There was a certain amount of Italian settlement, and an Italian minority still remains in Tripolitania. Libya is now a constitutional monarchy under King Idris I, the head of the Senussi, the Arab sect most fiercely and irreconcilably hostile to the Italians.

Oil has now been located west of Aujila, in Cyrenaica, and this may make a revolutionary change in the economic situation.

MAP 41

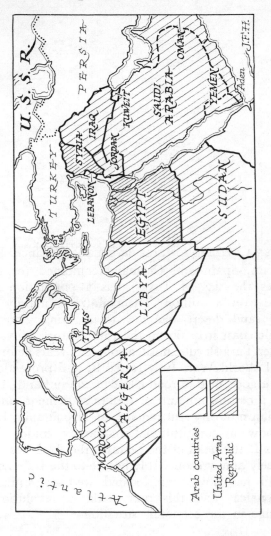

COLONEL NASSER'S VISION

MODERN POLITICAL and economic develop-
ment ignores the academic division of the world into
continents. France wishes to make Algeria part of
Europe. Colonel Nasser, as leader of the Arab world,
would like the whole of North Africa to be in close
union with Western Asia (i.e. with the Middle East)
an area extending from the Atlantic to the Persian
Gulf. The internal politics of the Arab countries, as
has been obvious in Iraq since the revolution of
1958, are very largely concerned with the struggle
between pro-Nasser and anti-Nasser elements. The
monarchies of Morocco, Libya and Saudi Arabia
tend to stand aloof from him, and so far only one of
the Arab republics, Syria, has accepted closer union
with Egypt. An Egyptian delegation took part in the
All-Africa Conference in December, 1958; and the
Afro-Asian People's Solidarity Council, on which
forty African and Asian peoples are represented, has
as one of its main aims "active help to the freedom
movements in the still dependent countries of Africa."

PART III
TOMORROW

MAP 42

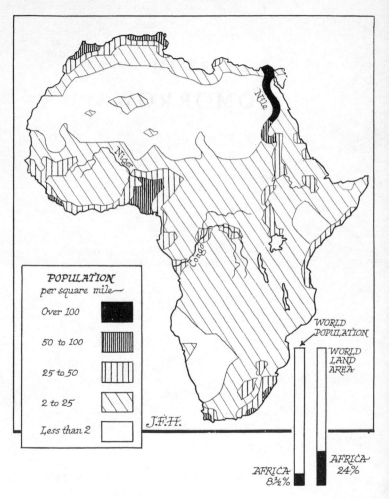

POPULATION
per square mile—

Over 100

50 to 100

25 to 50

2 to 25

Less than 2

Nile

Niger

Congo

J.F.H.

WORLD
POPULATION

WORLD
LAND
AREA

AFRICA
8½%

AFRICA
24%

MORE SETTLERS NEEDED?

THE ANSWER IS emphatically "Yes." It is a good many years now since Norman Leys, after years of service in Kenya, urged that what Africa most needed was numbers of *lay* missionaries—scientists, technical experts, skilled workmen of all kinds— men and women prepared to live and work with Africans on equal terms, to put their knowledge and skill at the Africans' disposal, to *help* (not "direct") in the colossal task of bringing African standards of living up to the level of Europe's; Europeans, in short, like Dr. Albert Schweitzer and Mr. Guy Clutton-Brock. Europeans owe that debt to Africans. And Africa—leaving out the great deserts—is under-populated. Three times the size of Europe it has less than a third of Europe's population. As another Kenya doctor[1] has written: "Only by breaking away from the evil heritage of the past, and by a *change of direction by men of all races*, can Africa find salvation."

[1] C. J. Wilson, *Before the White Man in Kenya.*

MAP 43

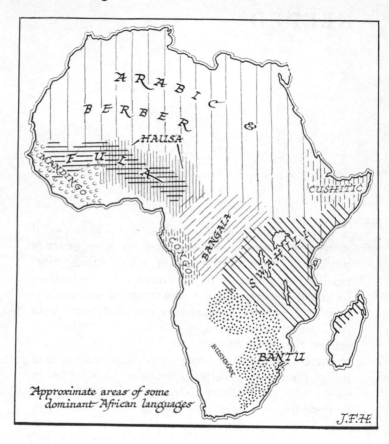

Approximate areas of some
dominant African languages

THE PROBLEM OF LANGUAGE

THIS IS A GROSSLY over-simplified map, showing the broad distribution of some main language-groups in Africa. These should be broken down into scores of languages, most of them of course, without any written alphabet as yet. (There are twenty different languages in Ghana alone.) Anthropologists in all parts of the continent are at work on this problem.

For practical purposes—commerce, education, administration—the languages of present-day Africa are Arabic, English, French, Swahili and Afrikaans. As we have seen, the new parliaments of Ghana and Nigeria carry on their debates in English; and those of the French republics in French. Swahili, the *lingua franca* of the East Coast, is a mixture of Arabic and Bantu. Afrikaans is confined to the Union of South Africa.

Like nationalists everywhere (e.g. in Ireland and India) African nationalists wish to preserve their languages. But if education, for instance, had to await the translation of essential textbooks into every African language the march of progress would be slowed down to a crawl. English and French will inevitably be used more and more. (Soviet broadcasts to Africa are in these two languages.)

MAP 44

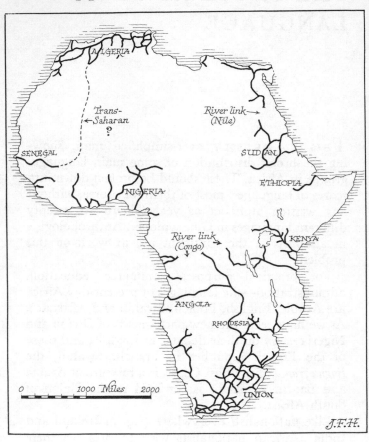

ALGERIA

Trans-
←Saharan
?

River link →
(Nile)

SENEGAL

SUDAN

ETHIOPIA

NIGERIA

River link
(Congo) →

KENYA

ANGOLA

RHODESIA

0   1000 *Miles* 2000

UNION

J.F.H.

THE PROBLEM OF TRANSPORT

AFRICA, IT IS scarcely surprising to learn, has fewer miles of railroad than any other continent. Only in the north (Morocco, Algeria, Tunis) and in the extreme south (the Union) is there anything like a developed network, with rather less elaborate systems in the other two "settler" areas, Kenya and Rhodesia. Cecil Rhodes' dream of a Cape-to-Cairo line was never realised. Such as they are, the railways, as is obvious from the map, have been constructed to feed particular ports.

All-weather roads may well play a bigger part than railways in the Africa of the future. Public work departments and laboratories in various territories are today studying road materials, soil mechanics, etc.

Air-lines, of course, now link the various parts of the continent. There must be many Africans to whom an aeroplane is a familiar sight who have never seen a railway train.

The Colonial Development Corporation, inaugurated by the 1945-50 Labour Government, has played an important part in various schemes of economic development in the British territories—transport, mining, agriculture, etc.

MAP 45

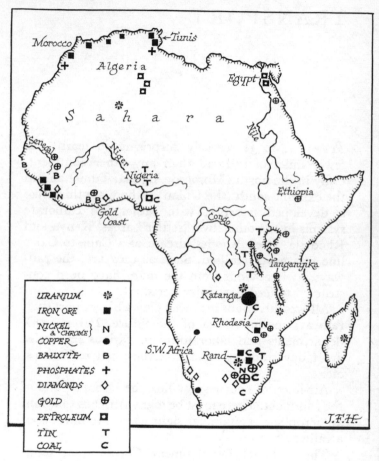

Morocco
Tunis
Algeria
Egypt
S a h a r a
Senegal
Niger
Nigeria
Ethiopia
B
B
N
B B
Gold
Coast
C
Congo
T
T
T
Tanganyika
Katanga
C
Rhodesia
N
S.W. Africa
Rand
C T
N
C
C
Nile

URANIUM ✳
IRON ORE ■
NICKEL & CHROME } N
COPPER ●
BAUXITE B
PHOSPHATES +
DIAMONDS ◇
GOLD ⊕
PETROLEUM ▢
TIN T
COAL C

J.F.H.

MINERAL WEALTH

GOLD WAS A MAJOR objective of the first European traders to West Africa, and it is still mined in Ghana (the Gold Coast). But the richest goldfields were only discovered in the late 19th century, on the Rand, in the Transvaal (and they were a primary cause of the Boer War). There is gold also in Kenya, Tanganyika, and Rhodesia. Kimberley was once the most important diamond field, but the largest fields now are in the Belgian Congo and in South-West Africa (held by the Union). The other most important metal area in Africa is the Katanga copper belt, divided between the Congo and N. Rhodesia.

In all these mining centres the labour is African, and a major problem results from the male populations of whole areas leaving their village to work, on two-or-three-year contracts, in the mines; doubly a problem because not only are the villages denuded of active workers, but the miners are brought into contact with "civilisation" at its rawest and crudest.

Great reserves of bauxite in Ghana and Guinea, and of iron ore in Mauritania and Liberia, have only just begun to be worked.

MAP 46

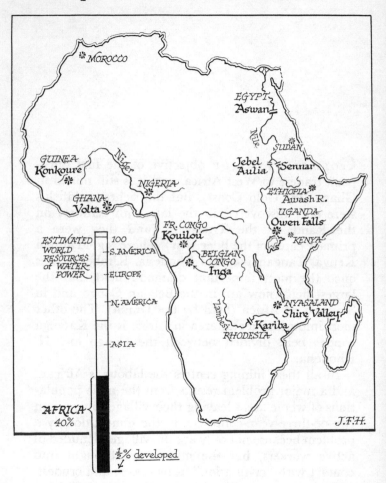

Morocco

EGYPT
Aswan

Nile

GUINEA
Konkouré

Niger

NIGERIA

GHANA
Volta

SUDAN

Jebel
Aulia

Sennar

ETHIOPIA
Awash R.

UGANDA
Owen Falls

ESTIMATED
WORLD
RESOURCES
of WATER-
POWER

100

S. AMERICA

EUROPE

N. AMERICA

ASIA

FR. CONGO
Kouilou

KENYA

BELGIAN
CONGO
Inga

Zambesi

NYASALAND
Shire Valley

Kariba

RHODESIA

AFRICA
40%

½% developed

J.F.H.

WATER AND WATER-POWER

AFRICA, IT IS estimated, has 40% of the water-power of the globe. Less than $\frac{1}{2}$% has so far been developed. Yet water, as a scientist has pointed out,[1] "is scanty in at least three-quarters of Africa south of the Sahara, and it would be no exaggeration to say that in more than half of the region water is the principal factor limiting all forms of human endeavour."

The map shows some of the principal centres of hydro-electric power, actually working or projected. As will be noted, the four great rivers—Nile, Niger, Congo and Zambesi—all come into this picture. The damming of these rivers not only means electric power, but water for irrigation; and it may be mentioned here that African agricultural production has increased by over half in the last twenty years, well above the world's average increase.

A scheme which might have had revolutionary results all over Africa was the Tanganyika Ground Nut Scheme (1947), which, "in spite of the failure of its main objective," says the scientist already quoted, "did much scientific work of a pioneering character."

[1] E. B. Worthington, *Science in the Development of Africa.*

MAP 47

Philippeville
Bougie
Algiers
Tangier
Casablanca
Tunis
Biskra
Gabes
Khouribga
MOROCCO
Tripoli
Touggourt
Hassi R'mel
Colomb-Béchar
Hassi Messaoud
Pipe-line
Tindouf
ALGERIA
SPAN. SAHARA
Edjelé
LIBYA
Tiguentourine
S a h a r a
Fort Gouraud
Proposed Trans-Saharan railway
Akjouit
MAURITANIA
HOGGAR
Senegal
NIGER
Dakar
Niger
FR. SUDAN
J.F.H.

Paris

FRANCE
on same scale.

Oil wells	◧
Oil concessions	▨
Phosphates	✕
Iron Ore	▲
Uranium	✳
Copper	▽

116

OPENING UP THE SAHARA

ONE UNSOLVED question on which scientists are
working is whether the dessication of the Sahara has
yet ceased—whether it and its surrounding regions
are drying up still further. However that may be the
Sahara has recently been found to contain liquid of
another sort, a sort especially valuable in the world
today—oil. In eastern Algeria oil-wells are actually
in production at Hassi Messaoud, Edgelé, and
Tiguentourine. A pipeline connects the former with
Touggourt, railhead of a line from Edgelé and Gabes,
in Tunisia. Oil is being searched for in a wide area
(see map).

Iron is also being worked, and uranium has been
discovered in the Hoggar, the volcanic massif in the
very centre of the Sahara.

MAP 48

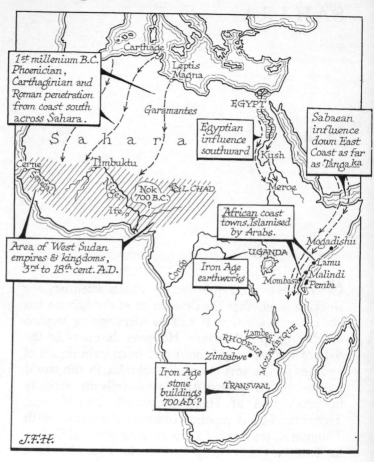

1st millenium B.C.
Phoenician,
Carthaginian and
Roman penetration
from coast south
across Sahara.

Carthage

Leptis
Magna

EGYPT

Garamantes

S a h a r a

Egyptian
influence
southward

Sabaean
influence
down East
Coast as far
as Tanga_ka_

Cerne

Timbuktu

Kush

Senegal

Ger

Nok
(700 B.C.)
?

L. CHAD

Ife

Meroe

African coast
towns, Islamised
by Arabs.

Area of West Sudan
empires & kingdoms,
3rd to 18th cent. A.D.

Congo

UGANDA

Iron Age
earthworks

Mogadishu

Lamu

Malindi

Mombasa

Pemba

Zambezi

RHODESIA

Zimbabwe

MOZAMBIQUE

Iron Age
stone
buildings
700 A.D.?

TRANSVAAL

J.F.H.

DIGGING UP AFRICA'S PAST

THE AFRICA OF the future will know a great deal
more about the Africa of the past. Although relatively little systematic excavation has been done,
archaeologists have already proved that Africa is
extremely rich in evidences of the Stone Age, the
Neolothic and the Iron Ages. (And "archaeology in
this letterless continent," remarks Basil Davidson,
"is concerned with 'pre-history' right up to the 18th
century.") Until recently, moreover, neither primitive Africans nor civilised (?) settlers showed much
respect for the remains of ancient cultures, some rock-
paintings, according to E. B. Worthington, having
been used for 0·22 rifle practice.

The map shows a few of the main areas and
objectives on which archaeological work has begun,
or is planned.

MAP 49

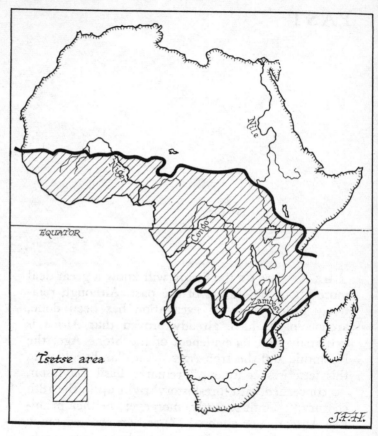

EQUATOR

Tsetse area

J.F.H.

MOSQUITO AND TSETSE

Two of man's deadliest enemies in Africa—much more dangerous than lions, rhinosceri or buffalo—are insects: the malaria mosquito and the tsetse-fly. "The mosquito is bad enough," writes Sir Julian Huxley,[1] but malaria does not drive cultivation out of a country like the fly-disease of cattle, nor does it kill humans wholesale, like the tsetse, by sleeping-sickness. . . . And there is not merely one, but half a dozen kinds of tsetse-fly;[2] and several of them will convey the trypanosomes of cattle disease or of sleeping-sickness with complete impartiality, either separately or both at once. Tsetse live largely on game. But you cannot, even if you wanted to, exterminate all the game in the country. . . . Tsetse live chiefly in bush. But you cannot readily destroy tracts of bush as big as France."

The map shows the Tsetse Belt. But there are areas within it free from the fly, which is unable to live in high altitudes (anything over 2,000 metres) or in grassy or cultivated areas, free from bush, or in dense forest. . . . Laboratories in Europe as well as in Africa are working intensively on tsetse control.

A note on the mosquito: "The most dangerous agency for carrying mosquitoes or the diseases they transmit about the world today," E. B. Worthington reminds us, "is the aeroplane."

[1] *Africa View.*   [2] E. B. Worthington says there are twenty-one.

MAP 50

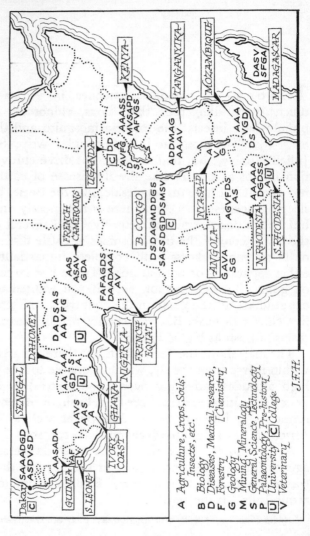

A Agriculture, Crops, Soils.
   Insects, etc.
B Biology
D Diseases, Medical research,
F Forestry   [Chemistry]
G Geology
M Mining, Mineralogy
S General Science, Technology
P Palaeontology, Pre-history,
Ⓤ University Ⓒ College
V Veterinary

J.F.H.

SCIENCE, SCIENCE, SCIENCE . . .

THIS, ALTHOUGH not all African nationalists may realise it, is perhaps the most important map in this book. It shows, in a cross-central section of the continent, the scientific work now being done—the institutes, research stations, technical services operating in the several territories, roughly classified in their various groups.

What each initial letter represents may be gauged by two or three specimen descriptions from the list given by E. B. Worthington in his *Science in the Development of Africa*:—

Belgian Congo: *Comité Special du Katanga*, Elizabethville. 45 scientists. Cartography, geology and mining, hydrology, agriculture, forestry and animal production.

Ivory Coast: *Institut d'Enseignment et des Recherches Tropicales*. 13 scientists. Botany, agricultural and medical entomology.

Rhodesia: *Grasslands Agricultural Research Station*. 9 scientists. Pasture research and animal husbandry.

Mozambique: *Missao de Combate as Tripanosomiasis*. 21 scientists. Human and animal trypanosomiasis and tsetse flies. With 3 sub-stations for entomological work and 5 for the control of disease.

This is the work which is going to enable Africa to take its place in the 20th-century world. And note: *some of these scientists are Africans, and their number is increasing.*

INDEX

The numbers are of maps, but the entries refer to the letterpress opposite the map as well as to the map itself.